My Science Project

by Sayuri Naka

Lloyd Kajikawa
Illustrated by Sue Mell

A Harcourt Achieve Imprint

www.Rigby.com
1-800-531-5015

September 16

Today my teacher, Ms. Johnson, announced that our class is going to have a science fair. Everyone in my class is going to pick a topic and create a science project. Ms. Johnson also wants each of us to keep a journal while we are working on our projects. I love science, so I'm really excited! We spent the last ten minutes of science class talking about ideas.

There's a lot to do before the fair, and I can't begin until I choose my topic! How will I ever choose just one?

Here are my ideas:

the moon

electricity

growing plants

waves in the ocean

September 23

It's been a whole week, and I haven't chosen my topic yet. Monique, who is my best friend, came over today to help me think of ideas. Monique is in my science class, too, and she chose her topic last week. Her project will be on clouds and weather. I don't know how she decided so quickly. But she says that when she has to decide something, first she makes a list of her choices, so I decided to make a list of some science questions. It is a very long list!

This is Monique and me.

But I still can't make up my mind! I stuck my list on the refrigerator with a magnet so that I can look at it every morning while I eat breakfast.

- How do snowflakes form?
- What is gravity?
- Why do bears sleep through the winter?
- How does a bone become a fossil?
- How do whales breathe?
- What is a tornado?
- Why do birds sing?
- How does a computer work?

September 30

Guess what? My younger brothers, who are rarely helpful, accidentally helped me pick a topic for my science project! They were running around and Jiro bumped into the refrigerator. He wasn't hurt, but he knocked off all of the magnets and tore my list. I was angry at first, especially when they started playing with the magnets instead of fixing my paper and replacing it on the refrigerator. But then I watched them connect the magnets together like a train. Then they made one magnet push another one around the table.

That gave me a great idea for my project.
And it had been on top of my list the whole time!
I decided to do my project on magnets.

When I saw my brothers playing
with magnets, I knew that how
magnets work was a good topic.

October 2

I can't believe that the science fair is only about a month away. Dad bought all sorts of magnets for me to use. I took a bar magnet around the house and had fun trying to stick it on different things made of metal. In the kitchen, it stuck to the refrigerator, the stove, a knife, and our forks and spoons. I tried to put it on one of our frying pans, but it didn't stick. I didn't know why that happened, but Mom told me that the frying pan is made of **aluminum.**

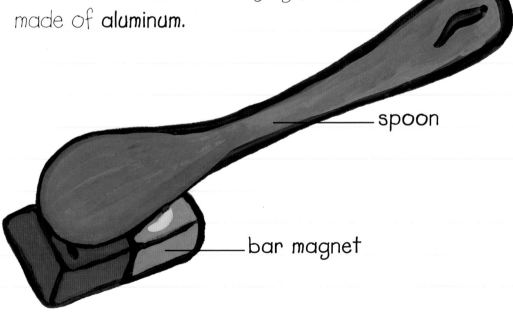

spoon

bar magnet

Then I put the magnet on an aluminum soda can, and it didn't stick there either. I guess aluminum is one of those metals that doesn't **attract,** or pull closer to, magnets.

My magnet didn't stick to the frying pan or the soda can.

October 5

I looked up magnets on the Internet. I learned some neat things that I didn't know before. I found out that magnets are surrounded by a force called a **magnetic field.** I think that this is what pushes away some objects and pulls other objects closer. One Web site said that magnets have two opposite **poles,** a north pole and a south pole, just like Earth. The magnetic field flows out of the magnet from the north pole and back into the magnet at the south pole.

north pole   south pole

north pole

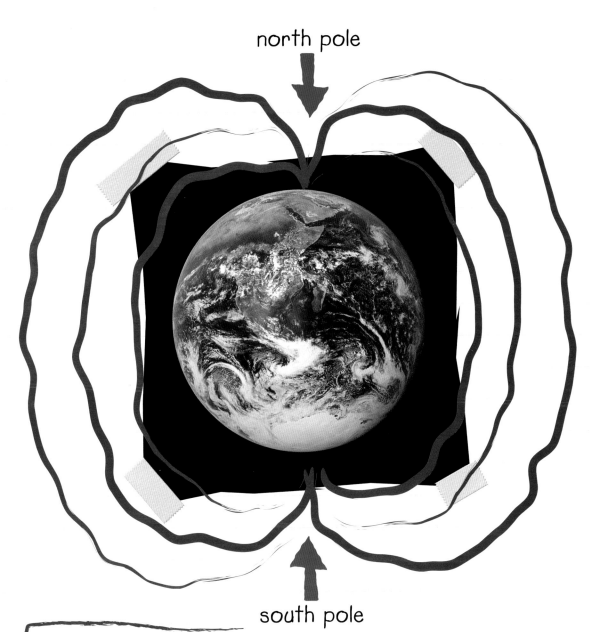

south pole

This is the magnetic field
that goes around Earth.

October 10

I'm still trying to figure out how to make magnets into a good project. Dad helped me by teaching me a trick with my magnets' north and south poles. He told me that if you hang a small magnet by a string, the magnet will turn so that its north pole faces north and its south pole faces south.

I tried this with two bar magnets, using Mom's **compass** to figure out the directions. I wrote an N on each north pole, and an S on each south pole. When I put two north poles or two south poles together, they pushed each other away.

When I brought one north pole and one south pole near each other, the magnets stuck together.

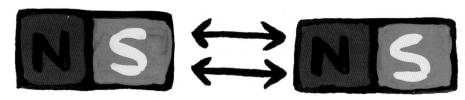

October 14

Our projects were discussed in class today. It was fun to hear about what everyone is doing. Of course, we didn't want to give too much information about our projects because we all want them to be a surprise on the day of the science fair.

I think Monique's project on clouds will be terrific. Carlo is doing something with fireflies. That will be really cool, too, and I can't wait to see it! Sara is working with Habib on a project about gravity.

Monique's project has many clouds.

Carlo's project is
about fireflies.

Sara and Habib
are working on
a project
about gravity.

November 1

Wow! There's only one more week until the science fair! Today Ms. Johnson met with us and gave us the floor plan that shows where each of our projects will be. I'm so excited because mine will be next to Monique's!

Ms. Johnson said that it's important to practice before the science fair. I'm going to set up my project at home and have my mom preview everything. That way, things will go smoothly.

Science Fair Floor Plan

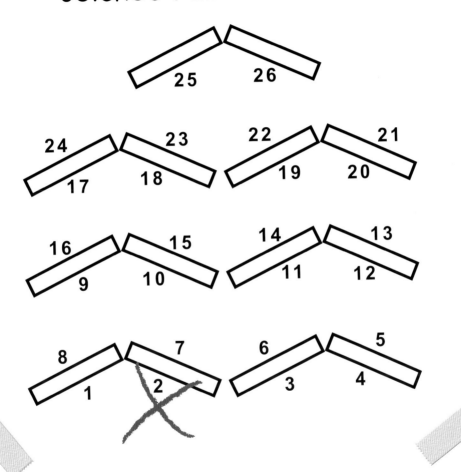

The X is where my project will be.

November 4

I read on the Internet that a good display has things for people to touch and do. I recall that I like museums better when I can push buttons or do something, so I decided to have things for people to do, too.

I'll have objects that people can stick magnets on. I'll also have paper clips on a piece of paper that kids can try to move with a magnet from under the paper. I'll also have some magnet tricks and lots of pictures that show magnets sticking to different things. I think it's going to be fun.

Dad is going to help me pretest my magnet tricks, and Mom is going to help me set up my project at school. I'm going to have so much fun showing everyone how magnets work!

November 8

I'm at the science fair right now! I thought that I'd bring my journal and write about the other projects I see so that I don't forget.

Monique's project is really neat. She used lots of cotton to show what the different kinds of clouds look like.

Monique

The fireflies project assembled by Carlo is also great! He has some really cool pictures that explain how fireflies light up. I hope that everyone likes my project.

Carlo

November 9

The science fair was great, and I can hardly believe it's over. Everyone who came to my booth enjoyed watching me do magnet tricks. I put a round magnet on top of a piece of paper that I was holding in one hand. With my other hand, I used a bar magnet under the piece of paper to move the round magnet around. Everyone thought that the trick was neat!

I was so happy when Ms. Johnson told me that my project was great. I can't wait to do another one next year! I already have an idea for a topic. I think that Monique will be very surprised!

Glossary

aluminum metal that does not attract magnets
attract to pull something closer
compass an instrument that shows directions
magnetic field the area of force around a
magnet that attracts certain metals
poles the opposite ends of magnets

Index

bar magnet 8, 13, 22
compass 13
magnetic field 10–11
poles 10–11, 12–13

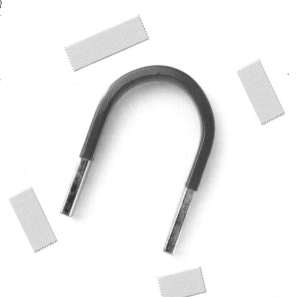